EXPLORING
BOSNIA AND HERZEGOVINA

A JOURNEY THROUGH HISTORY, CULTURE, AND NATURE

BY

WILLIAM JONES

2024

Exploring Bosnia and Herzegovina: A Journey through History, Culture, and Nature by William Jones

This book edition was created and published by Mamba Press

©MambaPress 2024. All Rights Reserved.

Contents

Preface

Welcome, fellow traveler, to the pages of this guide, where words weave tales of Bosnia and Herzegovina, a land etched with stories that span the epochs of time. My name is William Jones, your humble guide in this exploration of a country that holds the whispers of empires, the echoes of battles, and the warm embrace of tradition. As you embark on this journey with me, let us traverse the mosaic of Bosnia and Herzegovina, a destination that invites you not merely to witness its wonders but to become a part of its narrative.

Nestled in the heart of Southeastern Europe, Bosnia and Herzegovina offer a tapestry of experiences that unfold against a backdrop of history, culture, and natural beauty. It is a country that has endured the ebb and flow of civilizations, emerging resilient and steadfast. In these pages, you will find not just a travel guide but a chronicle of discovery, a map to navigate through the layers of an ancient land.

As you turn the pages, picture yourself standing in Sarajevo, where the threads of East and West intertwine, and each cobblestone echoes with the footsteps of centuries past. Sense the anticipation as you approach Mostar, a city where a singular bridge, the Stari Most, stands as a testament to both engineering marvels and the indomitable spirit of its people. Wander through the quiet streets of Jajce, where waterfalls cascade in harmony with history, or traverse the hills of Visegrad, a town echoing with the tales of empires.

Bosnia and Herzegovina, a land once torn by conflict, now beckon travelers with open arms and an invitation to partake in its healing embrace. The cities, villages, and landscapes are not merely waypoints; they are chapters in an unfolding story. The stories of resilience, courage, and an unyielding spirit that define the soul of this nation.

As we delve into the heart of this guide, consider it not just a manual but a companion, a storyteller, and a curator of experiences. Picture yourself in the bustling markets of Sarajevo, the aroma of grilled cevapi wafting through the air, or feel the cool mist from the cascading waters of Kravice Waterfalls on your face. Let the vibrant hues of Blagaj, with its turquoise river and historic Dervish house, paint an image in your mind.

The journey is not just about the destinations but the people who call this land home. Meet the locals, share in their stories, and savor the moments that reveal the beating heart of Bosnia and Herzegovina. Here, hospitality is not a gesture but a way of life, where strangers are welcomed as friends, and every conversation is an exchange of cultural riches.

In the chapters that follow, you'll find practical advice on navigating the cities, understanding the historical context, and savoring the flavors that define Bosnian cuisine. But beyond the practicalities, let this guide be an invitation to immerse yourself fully in the experience. Allow the ancient stones of Mostar to speak to you, let the call to prayer in Sarajevo resonate within, and find solace in the serene landscapes that stretch across the countryside.

So, as you embark on this odyssey through Bosnia and Herzegovina, let curiosity be your compass, and may each step deepen your connection with this extraordinary land. Welcome to a journey where the past and present intertwine, where every corner holds a story, and where, with an open heart, you become not just a traveler but a participant in the ongoing narrative of a nation. The stage is set, the stories await – let the adventure unfold.

Introduction

Welcome, dear reader, to the gateway of a journey, where the pages of this guide unfurl like a treasure map, revealing the wonders that await in Bosnia and Herzegovina. As we embark on this odyssey, envision the anticipation of a new chapter, a story woven through the fabric of time, where ancient history, vibrant culture, and untouched landscapes converge.

Bosnia and Herzegovina, a name that echoes through the corridors of history, is a land of contrasts and complexity. Tucked away in the heart of Southeastern Europe, it's a country that has witnessed the rise and fall of empires, the tumult of wars, and the resilient spirit of its people emerging victorious against all odds. Today, it beckons travelers with open arms, inviting them to explore its hidden gems, engage with its diverse communities, and soak in the breathtaking beauty that lies around every corner.

Imagine standing in Sarajevo, the capital that proudly wears the scars of its past and the aspirations of its future. This city, where East meets West, is a living testament to the confluence of cultures, religions, and histories. As you wander through its streets, you'll find yourself transported through time, the echoes of Ottoman rule mingling with Austro-Hungarian architecture, and the call to prayer harmonizing with the hum of a bustling market.

Mostar, a city that dances on the edge of the Neretva River, beckons you to cross the iconic Stari Most – a bridge that not only spans the water but also bridges the gap between tradition and modernity. Here, the vibrant bazaar invites you to lose yourself in a maze of cobblestone streets, where artisans ply their trade and the aroma of freshly baked burek hangs in the air.

Jajce, with its cascading waterfalls, seems to be a place untouched by the hands of time. It's a city where nature and history entwine, inviting you to explore the remnants of medieval fortifications and feel the cool mist on your face as you stand before the roaring Pliva Falls.

But beyond the well-trodden paths lie gems like Travnik, a town that whispers tales of Ottoman glory in the rustling leaves of its plane trees. Traverse its cobbled streets, and you'll discover the legacy of grand viziers and sip coffee in courtyards where history itself seems to linger.

Banja Luka, the laid-back capital of Republika Srpska, unfolds with an air of tranquility. Parks, boulevards, and a lively cafe culture characterize this city, where time seems to slow down, inviting you to immerse yourself in its easygoing charm.

And then there's Tuzla, a city built upon the salt of the earth. Dive into the industrial beauty of its salt pans, where the crystalline structures glisten in the sunlight, and feel the soothing waters of the Pannonian Lakes, providing respite from the hustle and bustle of urban life.

Visegrad, perched on the Drina River, takes you on a journey through history, with the Mehmed Paša Sokolović Bridge standing tall as a silent witness to centuries gone by. The town exudes a sense of timelessness, where the past and present coexist in harmony.

As we traverse through this land, we encounter Srebrenica, a place that demands reflection. The wounds of its past are still healing, and the haunting Srebrenica-Potocari Memorial Center serves as a somber reminder of the atrocities committed during the Bosnian War. It is a place where history confronts you with its harsh reality, urging you to remember and learn.

Bihac, situated on the banks of the Una River, is the gateway to Una National Park, a haven for nature enthusiasts. Explore dense forests, pristine rivers, and cascading waterfalls, and let the untouched beauty of this national park leave an indelible mark on your soul.

Kravice Waterfalls, a natural spectacle near Ljubuski, invites you to witness the sheer power and beauty of nature. Immerse yourself in the refreshing waters, surrounded by lush greenery, and feel the magic of this enchanting oasis.

Blagaj, where rivers and mysticism converge, paints a picture of tranquility. The Buna River springs forth from a cavern at the base of a cliff, forming a turquoise pool that mirrors the surrounding beauty. Visit the historic Dervish house and absorb the serene atmosphere that permeates this mystical place.

Pocitelj, a step back in time, unfolds as an open-air museum. The medieval architecture, perched on a hillside, provides panoramic views of the Neretva River. Wander through its narrow streets, adorned with stone houses, and let the ancient stones speak to you.

The National Museum of Bosnia and Herzegovina in Sarajevo serves as a gateway to the country's past. Dive into the exhibits that unravel the complex tapestry of Bosnia and Herzegovina's history, from prehistoric times to the present day.

Amidst the exploration of cities and historical sites, don't forget to savor the heart and soul of Bosnia and Herzegovina – its cuisine. From the succulent cevapi to the aromatic burek, the culinary journey is a celebration of flavors that reflect the country's diverse influences.

And when you've had your fill of cityscapes and cultural explorations, it's time to embrace the great outdoors. Bosnia and Herzegovina offer a plethora of outdoor adventures, from hiking in the Dinaric Alps to rafting in the wild rivers. The landscapes are a playground for those seeking an adrenaline rush and a sanctuary for those desiring tranquility.

In these pages, you'll find practical tips on navigating the cities, understanding the historical context, and indulging in the diverse offerings of Bosnian cuisine. But beyond the logistics, consider this guide an invitation to immerse yourself fully in the experience. Let the ancient stones of Mostar speak to you, allow the call to prayer in Sarajevo to resonate within, and find solace in the serene landscapes that stretch across the countryside.

As you embark on this odyssey through Bosnia and Herzegovina, let curiosity be your compass, and may each step deepen your connection with this extraordinary land. Welcome to a journey where the past and present intertwine, where every corner holds a story, and where, with an open heart, you become not just a traveler but a participant in the ongoing narrative of a nation.

The stage is set, the stories await – let the adventure unfold.

Chapter 1

Sarajevo – Where East Meets West

Welcome to Sarajevo, a city where the echoes of history reverberate through its winding streets, and where the meeting of East and West creates a tapestry of cultures, traditions, and stories. As you step into this vibrant urban center, prepare to be enchanted by a city that has endured the tumultuous currents of time, emerging as a testament to resilience, diversity, and a rich cultural heritage.

Sarajevo, the capital and heart of Bosnia and Herzegovina, is more than just a geographical point on the map; it is a living chronicle of centuries gone by. Imagine strolling through the Baščaršija, the city's historical bazaar, where the scent of grilled cevapi fills the air, and the rhythmic beats of coppersmiths shaping their wares create a symphony of craftsmanship. Here, the centuries-old architecture whispers tales of the Ottoman era, inviting you to traverse through time.

The city's soul is shaped by the Miljacka River, which weaves its way through the urban landscape, dividing Sarajevo into distinct neighborhoods. As you cross its bridges, you'll find yourself transported between worlds, from the Ottoman-influenced Baščaršija to the Austro-Hungarian elegance of Marijin Dvor. Each step in Sarajevo is a journey through history, where minarets punctuate the skyline alongside cathedrals and synagogues, harmonizing in a visual representation of the city's religious diversity.

Begin your exploration in Bascarsija, the heart of Sarajevo's historic center. The cobblestone streets, lined with shops and cafes, exude a timeless charm. Picture yourself navigating through the narrow alleys, where each turn reveals hidden gems – a centuries-old fountain, a traditional Bosnian house, or a tucked-away courtyard where locals engage in animated conversations over a cup of strong Bosnian coffee.

As you delve deeper into Baščaršija, let the aroma of Bosnian coffee guide you to one of the many traditional kafanas. Sit beneath the shaded awnings, sip your coffee slowly, and absorb the rhythm of life around you. This is not just a coffee break; it's an immersion into the social fabric of Sarajevo, where time seems to stand still.

The Sebilj, a wooden fountain at the heart of Baščaršija, serves as a meeting point and a symbol of the city's endurance. Legend has it that if you drink from the Sebilj, you will return to Sarajevo. Take a moment to quench your thirst here, and perhaps, like many before you, you'll find yourself irresistibly drawn back to this city of stories.

Venture towards the Gazi Husrev-beg Mosque, an architectural masterpiece that has watched over Sarajevo since the 16th century. Its intricate calligraphy and geometric patterns are a testament to the artistic achievements of the Ottoman Empire. Step inside, where the air is filled with a sense of serenity, and witness the interplay of light and shadow dancing on the mosque's ornate walls.

A short walk from the mosque leads you to the Morica Han, a 16th-century caravanserai that once hosted traveling merchants. Today, it houses a charming restaurant where you can savor Bosnian delicacies in an ambiance that transports you back to the days of the Silk Road. The Morica Han encapsulates the essence of Sarajevo – a city where history and modernity coexist seamlessly.

As the day unfolds, make your way to the Latin Bridge, a seemingly unassuming structure that played a pivotal role in the events that ignited World War I. It was here, in 1914, that Archduke Franz Ferdinand of Austria was assassinated, setting in motion a chain of events that would shape the course of history. The bridge, with its understated elegance, stands as a silent witness to the complexities of human destiny.

The Jewish Cemetery on the hillside is a poignant reminder of Sarajevo's multicultural past. Here, tombstones of different shapes and sizes tell the stories of generations that lived side by side, fostering a harmonious coexistence that has left an indelible mark on the city's identity.

As you ascend to the Yellow Fortress (Zuta Tabija), perched on a hill overlooking the city, the panorama of Sarajevo unfolds beneath you. The juxtaposition of minarets, church spires, and modern skyscrapers against the backdrop of rolling hills captures the essence of a city where East truly meets West. Take a moment to absorb the view, and you'll realize that Sarajevo is not just a city; it's a living mosaic, each piece contributing to the vibrancy of the whole.

As evening descends, the Sebilj Square comes alive with a different energy. Join the locals as they gather for the evening promenade, known as šetnja. The streets are illuminated, and the sounds of laughter and music fill the air. Cafes spill onto the sidewalks, and the city transforms into a lively stage where the day's stories continue to unfold.

For a taste of Sarajevo's nightlife, venture to Bascarsija's surrounding neighborhoods, such as Ferhadija and Titova Streets, where an array of bars and pubs cater to diverse tastes. Whether you're seeking a quiet corner for conversation or a vibrant dance floor, Sarajevo has a spot for every nocturnal adventurer.

And then there's the culinary tapestry of Sarajevo, a feast for the senses. Sample cevapi, minced meat grilled to perfection and served with somun, a traditional Bosnian bread. Try burek, a flaky pastry filled with meat, cheese, or potatoes, and let the flavors transport you to a world where each bite tells a story of centuries past.

End your day at one of Sarajevo's traditional inns, known as konak or han. Nestled in the heart of Baščaršija, these accommodations offer more than just a place to rest; they provide an opportunity to immerse yourself in the city's hospitality. Picture yourself in a cozy room, adorned with oriental carpets and vintage furniture, where the echoes of history linger in the air. As you retire for the night, you'll find that Sarajevo is not merely a destination; it's an experience that leaves an indelible mark on your soul.

In Sarajevo, East meets West not only in the architectural marvels that dot the city but also in the spirit of its people. It's a place where history is not confined to textbooks but lives and breathes in the rhythm of everyday life. So, as you navigate through the enchanting alleys of Baščaršija, let the stories of Sarajevo seep into your consciousness. For in this city, where East meets West, every corner is a portal to a world where the past and present dance in harmony, inviting you to become part of the timeless narrative of Sarajevo.

Chapter 2
Mostar – The Stari Most and Beyond

Welcome to Mostar, a city where the Neretva River flows with stories, and the iconic Stari Most stands as a symbol of resilience, beauty, and the enduring spirit of Bosnia and Herzegovina. As you step into this enchanting city, you'll find yourself captivated not only by the architectural marvels that grace its skyline but also by the warmth of its people and the tales that echo through its cobbled streets.

Begin your exploration in the heart of Mostar's Old Bazaar, a labyrinth of narrow alleys, bustling with the energy of shopkeepers, artisans, and visitors alike. The scent of freshly baked bread mingles with the aroma of Turkish coffee, creating an olfactory symphony that envelops you as you traverse through the centuries-old marketplace. Baazar Kujundžiluk, the main street of the bazaar, is a kaleidoscope of colors, with shops offering traditional handicrafts, intricately designed copperware, and vibrant textiles that mirror the city's rich cultural tapestry.

Take a moment to absorb the vibrant atmosphere, where the buzz of commerce intermingles with the strains of traditional Bosnian music. As you wander, you'll encounter locals engaged in animated conversations, their laughter echoing off the stone walls. This is Mostar – a city where the past and present coalesce seamlessly, inviting you to become a participant in its living history.

The Stari Most, or Old Bridge, is the crown jewel of Mostar, and its silhouette graces postcards, capturing the imagination of all who behold it. As you approach the bridge, let the gentle hum of the Neretva River guide you. The cobalt blue waters shimmer beneath the arched expanse of the Stari Most, a testament to the architectural brilliance of the Ottoman Empire. This 16th-century marvel connects the two halves of Mostar – the Muslim-influenced east and the predominantly Croat west.

Stand at the foot of the bridge and gaze up at its weathered stones, each one carrying the weight of centuries. Feel the vibrations beneath your feet as locals and daring divers alike traverse the Stari Most, a tradition that has endured for generations. The bridge is not merely a structure; it's a living, breathing entity that has withstood the tests of time, including the devastating war of the 1990s.

For a more intimate view of the Stari Most, climb the cobbled streets that lead to the Koski Mehmed Pasha Mosque. The minaret offers a panoramic vista of Mostar's skyline, with the bridge taking center stage. Here, the city unfolds like a storybook, with terracotta roofs and slender minarets punctuating the landscape. As the call to prayer resonates through the air, you'll find yourself immersed in the spiritual ambiance that has shaped the soul of Mostar for centuries.

Wander towards the historic Bazar Kujundžiluk, where the bridge casts its reflection on the Neretva River. In the evening, the Stari Most is bathed in the warm glow of streetlights, creating a scene straight out of a fairytale. Cafes along the riverbanks offer the perfect vantage point to witness this magical transformation. Imagine sipping Bosnian coffee or enjoying a glass of local wine as you absorb the enchanting view, the Stari Most becoming a bridge not just between two riverbanks but between the realms of reality and dreams.

As you explore the west side of Mostar, you'll encounter the Croats' influence on the city's architecture and way of life. The Catholic Church of St. Peter and Paul, with its neoclassical facade, stands as a testament to the city's religious diversity. Wander through the alleys adorned with street art, and you'll find yourself in a neighborhood where history is etched not only in stone but also in the vibrant murals that grace the walls.

The Museum of War and Genocide Victims provides a sobering glimpse into Mostar's recent past, offering a comprehensive narrative of the city's experiences during the Bosnian War. The exhibits, testimonials, and artifacts present a poignant reminder of the resilience and strength of Mostar's inhabitants. It's a place that invites reflection and underscores the importance of remembrance in understanding the complexities of Bosnia and Herzegovina's history.

Beyond the historical sites, Mostar beckons with culinary delights that reflect the region's diverse influences. Sample ćevapi, a dish consisting of minced meat kebabs served with somun bread, or indulge in traditional Bosnian sweets like baklava and tufahija. The aroma of grilled meats and freshly baked pastries wafts through the air, inviting you to savor the flavors that define Mostar's gastronomic identity.

For a leisurely meal with a view, choose a restaurant perched along the Neretva River, where you can dine on terraces overlooking the Stari Most. Imagine sipping a glass of local wine as the sun sets, casting a golden hue on the bridge and the river below. The evening lights come alive, and the reflections dance on the water's surface, creating a scene that transcends the ordinary.

No visit to Mostar is complete without witnessing the traditional diving spectacle from the Stari Most. Local daredevils, known as Mostari, take the plunge from the bridge's apex, showcasing a centuries-old tradition that combines skill, bravery, and a touch of showmanship. The Neretva River, though chilly, becomes a stage for these acrobatic feats, and the applause from onlookers reverberates through the city.

For a deeper understanding of Mostar's cultural heritage, attend a traditional Bosnian music or dance performance. The city's artistic scene is alive with the sounds of sevdah, a genre of music that evokes the soulful essence of Bosnian folklore. Whether in a cozy tavern or an open-air venue, let the melodies of sevdah transport you to a realm where emotions are expressed through song and dance.

As night falls, Mostar's bridges and cobblestone streets take on a mystical quality. The illuminated Stari Most becomes a beacon, guiding you through the city's nocturnal wonders. Explore the city's vibrant nightlife by visiting one of the cafes, bars, or clubs that line the riverbanks. Engage in conversation with locals, share stories, and immerse yourself in the convivial atmosphere that defines Mostar after dark.

Consider staying in a traditional guesthouse or boutique hotel, where the charm of Mostar's history is seamlessly woven into the fabric of your accommodation. Picture yourself waking up to the sounds of the Neretva River outside your window and stepping onto a balcony with views of the Stari Most. It's not just a place to rest; it's a continuation of the Mostar experience, where the city's stories linger in the air.

As you bid farewell to Mostar, know that you carry with you not just memories of a city with a breathtaking bridge but a profound connection to a place where history, culture, and the indomitable spirit of its people converge. Mostar, with its Stari Most and beyond, invites you to become a part of its narrative, to tread its cobbled streets, and to leave a piece of your heart in a city where every corner tells a tale of resilience, beauty, and the enduring bridge between past and present.

Chapter 3
Jajce – The City of Waterfalls

Welcome to Jajce, a hidden gem in the heart of Bosnia and Herzegovina that unfolds like a fairytale. As you approach this enchanting city, nestled amidst rolling hills and dense forests, you'll soon discover why Jajce is hailed as the "City of Waterfalls." Prepare to be captivated not just by the beauty of nature but by the rich history that permeates the air and the warm hospitality that defines the spirit of this charming Bosnian destination.

The journey to Jajce takes you through picturesque landscapes, winding roads, and quaint villages. The anticipation builds as you catch glimpses of the Pliva River winding its way through the lush greenery. And then, suddenly, the city appears – a medieval marvel with stone walls, red-tiled roofs, and a majestic waterfall that graces the heart of Jajce.

Start your exploration in the city center, where the sound of rushing water becomes your guide. The Pliva River splits into multiple cascades, creating a symphony of nature that reverberates through the cobblestone streets. The most striking of these waterfalls is the Pliva Waterfall, where the river takes a dramatic 17-meter plunge into the Vrbas River below. It's a sight that stops you in your tracks, inviting you to witness the sheer force and beauty of nature.

The old town of Jajce, with its medieval fortress, beckons you to step back in time. Wander through the cobbled streets, where stone houses and quaint cafes line the way. The scent of freshly baked pastries mingles with the earthy aroma of coffee, creating an inviting atmosphere that encourages you to explore at a leisurely pace.

Jajce's fortress, perched on a hill overlooking the town, unfolds as a living testament to the city's strategic importance throughout history. Climb to the top, where the panoramic view reveals the confluence of the Pliva and Vrbas rivers, creating an island upon which the old town sits. As you survey the landscape, let your imagination transport you to the medieval era, when Jajce was a formidable fortress at the crossroads of empires.

The fortress also houses the Museum of the Second Session of the National Liberation Army and Partisan Detachments of Bosnia and Herzegovina. The exhibits delve into the region's resistance against fascism during World War II, offering insights into a chapter of history that holds significant meaning for the locals. It's a poignant reminder of the sacrifices made for freedom and the enduring spirit of resilience that characterizes Jajce.

As you descend from the fortress, the sound of water beckons you towards the Pliva Lakes, a series of interconnected lakes formed by the river's flow. Picture yourself strolling along the shores, where the reflection of the surrounding greenery dances on the tranquil waters. The lakeside paths invite you to immerse yourself in the natural beauty, providing a serene escape from the bustle of everyday life.

At the lower end of the Pliva Lakes, the Small Pliva Waterfall adds to the city's aquatic charm. This picturesque cascade creates a gentle ambiance, perfect for a leisurely afternoon stroll. Find a quiet spot along the riverbank, perhaps on one of the inviting benches, and let the soothing sounds of flowing water and the rustling leaves envelop you in a moment of tranquility.

As you explore further, the historic Mlincici area reveals traditional watermills that once played a vital role in the city's economy. These charming structures, set against the backdrop of the Pliva River, stand as relics of a bygone era. Picture the waterwheels turning rhythmically, the sound of grinding grain filling the air, and the millers attending to their craft. It's a scene that transports you to a simpler time, where the flow of water shaped not only the landscape but also the livelihoods of Jajce's inhabitants.

The nearby St. Luke's Tower, part of the city's defensive walls, offers a different perspective of the Pliva Lakes and the surrounding countryside. Climb to the top, and you'll be rewarded with panoramic views that stretch across the undulating hills, making it clear why Jajce is often referred to as the "Bosnian Venice." Take a moment to absorb the beauty of the natural tapestry, where the lakes, forests, and waterfalls create a harmonious symphony of colors and textures.

For a deeper immersion into Jajce's religious and cultural heritage, visit the Church of the Holy Mary, a Catholic church dating back to the 14th century. The church's simple yet elegant design reflects the architectural influences of the medieval Bosnian Kingdom. Step inside, where the hushed atmosphere invites contemplation, and the centuries-old frescoes tell stories of faith and devotion.

Continue your exploration to the Grand Mosque of Jajce, a symbol of the city's diverse religious heritage. The mosque, constructed in the 16th century during the Ottoman era, stands as a reminder of the peaceful coexistence of different religious communities throughout history. As you stand in its courtyard, surrounded by the tranquility of the mosque and the murmur of the Pliva River, you'll witness the tangible expression of Jajce's harmonious blend of cultures.

For a taste of authentic Bosnian cuisine, the old town offers numerous options where you can savor traditional dishes. Picture yourself dining in a rustic restaurant, surrounded by stone walls and adorned with handmade textiles. Try local specialties such as begova čorba (a creamy chicken and okra soup) or japrak (grape leaves stuffed with minced meat and rice). Pair your meal with a glass of local wine or the renowned Bosnian coffee, served in traditional copper pots.

As the day unfolds into evening, follow the illuminated pathways along the Pliva River, where the city takes on a magical aura. The reflections of the streetlights dance on the water's surface, creating a serene ambiance that invites you to stroll along the riverside promenade. Explore the bridges that span the Pliva River, each offering a unique perspective of Jajce's cascading waterfalls and historic architecture.

Consider spending the night in one of the charming guesthouses or boutique hotels in the old town, where the medieval ambiance is complemented by modern comforts. Imagine waking up to the sound of rushing water and stepping onto a balcony with views of the Pliva Waterfall. It's not just a place to rest; it's an extension of the Jajce experience, where the city's natural beauty and cultural heritage become an integral part of your stay.

Jajce, the City of Waterfalls, invites you to embrace its unique blend of history, nature, and hospitality. As you bid farewell to this Bosnian gem, know that the memories of cascading waters, medieval fortifications, and warm encounters with locals will linger in your heart. Jajce, with its timeless charm and enchanting landscapes, unfolds as a chapter in your travel story, inviting you to return to its embrace whenever the call of waterfalls and history beckons.

Chapter 4

Travnik – A Glimpse into Ottoman Heritage

Welcome to Travnik, a city that whispers tales of Ottoman grandeur and cultural fusion. As you meander through its cobbled streets and historic squares, you'll find Travnik to be a living testament to a bygone era, where the echoes of Ottoman rule linger in the architecture, the cuisine, and the vibrant tapestry of daily life.

Travnik's journey through time begins in the 15th century when it served as the capital of the Ottoman province of Bosnia. As you approach the city, picture the imposing skyline dominated by the fortress of Travnik, perched on a hill with an unobstructed view of the surrounding landscape. The fortress, known as Stari Grad (Old Town), has stood witness to centuries of history, from the Ottoman period to the Austro-Hungarian rule, and offers a breathtaking panorama of the city below.

Start your exploration in the heart of Travnik, where the Grand Vizier's Mosque, also known as the Sulejmanija Mosque, unfolds as a masterpiece of Ottoman architecture. Step into its courtyard, where the intricate geometric patterns of the tiles and the gentle sound of a fountain create a serene atmosphere. The mosque, built in the 16th century, stands as a symbol of Travnik's cultural richness during the Ottoman era.

Wander through the narrow streets surrounding the mosque, where Ottoman-style houses with overhanging balconies and wooden window shutters line the way. As you explore, imagine the bustling markets that once thrived here, with merchants hawking spices, textiles, and handmade crafts. The aroma of freshly brewed coffee and the sound of artisans plying their trade would have filled the air, creating an ambiance that defined Travnik's Ottoman legacy.

The Travnik Fortress, with its well-preserved medieval walls and towers, offers not only a glimpse into the city's military past but also a panoramic view of Travnik's red-tiled roofs and minarets. Climb to the top, and you'll be rewarded with vistas that stretch across the rolling hills and the Lasva River valley. This vantage point provides insight into the city's strategic location and the influence of Ottoman rulers who sought to fortify Travnik against external threats.

Descend from the fortress into Travnik's historic center, where the Plava Voda Spring serves as a central gathering point. The spring, framed by a stone fountain and surrounded by lush greenery, is a place where locals and visitors alike come to refresh and socialize. Picture yourself joining the locals, filling your cup with the cool, clear water, and engaging in conversations that transcend language barriers. This simple act connects you to the heartbeat of Travnik, where the legacy of the Ottoman era lives on in everyday rituals.

For a deeper dive into Travnik's history, visit the Museum of Ivo Andrić, located in the house where the Nobel Prize-winning author once served as a diplomatic official during the Austro-Hungarian rule. The museum provides insight into Andrić's life and works, but it also serves as a window into the complex history of Bosnia and Herzegovina. As you peruse the exhibits, you'll gain a nuanced understanding of how the Ottoman legacy intersects with the region's more recent past.

Travnik's bustling bazaar, known as Bascarsija, is a vibrant marketplace that beckons you to explore its narrow alleys and vibrant stalls. Here, you'll find a variety of goods, from handmade crafts to locally produced textiles. Allow yourself to be enticed by the colors and textures that define Bosnian craftsmanship. Engage with the artisans, and you might find yourself leaving with a piece of Travnik to carry with you on your journey.

As you wander through the bazaar, the aroma of traditional Bosnian cuisine fills the air, drawing you towards the local eateries. Picture yourself seated in a cozy restaurant, the scent of slow-cooked stews and grilled meats tantalizing your senses. Sample local delicacies such as Bosanski lonac, a hearty meat and vegetable stew, or ćevapi, minced meat kebabs served with somun bread. The flavors are a fusion of Ottoman influences and local ingredients, creating a culinary experience that transports you to the crossroads of cultures.

The colorful Clock Tower, standing proudly in Travnik's city center, is not just a timekeeping device but a symbol of the city's Ottoman heritage. Built in the 18th century, the clock tower served as a focal point for the community, announcing prayer times and marking the rhythm of daily life. Picture yourself beneath the shadow of the clock tower, where the call to prayer once echoed through the city, uniting the residents in a shared sense of time and purpose.

For a moment of quiet contemplation, visit the tomb of the Ottoman governor Ishak-beg Finci. The tomb, nestled within a peaceful courtyard, is adorned with ornate calligraphy and geometric designs. As you stand before it, imagine the stories embedded in these stones – tales of leadership, culture, and a bygone era that still lingers in the architectural details.

The vibrant colors of Travnik's Old Bridge, also known as the Konjic Bridge, create a picturesque scene over the Lasva River. This Ottoman-era bridge, with its single arch and stone construction, is a testament to the engineering prowess of the time. Imagine yourself crossing this historic bridge, where the whispers of the past blend with the tranquil sounds of flowing water, creating a moment of reflection.

To delve deeper into the spiritual heritage of Travnik, visit the Alaca Mosque, a structure that combines elements of Ottoman and Islamic architecture. The mosque, with its graceful minaret and dome, invites you to step into a sanctuary of tranquility. As you enter, the hushed atmosphere and the intricate geometric patterns on the walls create a sense of reverence, offering a glimpse into the spiritual life of Travnik's residents.

In the evening, as the sun sets over the city, head to the Cafe Konak, an establishment that embodies the charm of Travnik's Ottoman legacy. Picture yourself on the terrace, where the soft glow of lanterns illuminates the historic surroundings. Sip on a cup of Turkish coffee or indulge in traditional Bosnian sweets as the city transforms into a canvas of golden hues. The rhythmic melodies of traditional Bosnian music may fill the air, creating an ambiance that seamlessly blends the old and the new.

Consider spending the night in one of the boutique hotels or guesthouses nestled within the historic center. Picture yourself in a room adorned with oriental rugs and antique furnishings, where the ambiance reflects the charm of Travnik's Ottoman past. As you retire for the night, the echoes of history linger in the air, inviting you to immerse yourself in the unique tapestry of Travnik's cultural heritage.

Travnik, with its Ottoman charm and cultural fusion, becomes not just a destination but a journey through time. As you bid farewell to this Bosnian gem, know that you carry with you not only memories of historical landmarks but a connection to a city where the past lives on in the everyday rituals of its people. Travnik invites you to become a part of its living history, to wander its cobbled streets, and to savor the legacy of the Ottoman era that endures in every corner of this captivating Bosnian city.

Chapter 5
Banja Luka – The Laid-Back Capital of Republika Srpska

Welcome to Banja Luka, the laid-back capital of Republika Srpska, where the easygoing pace of life intertwines with a rich cultural tapestry. As you step into this city, nestled along the banks of the Vrbas River, you'll find Banja Luka to be a destination that invites you to unwind, explore, and embrace the charm of its diverse heritage.

Begin your journey in the city center, where the Kastel Fortress stands as a silent guardian overlooking the Vrbas River. This medieval fortress, with its stone walls and towers, exudes a timeless elegance. Picture yourself strolling through its courtyard, where the air is filled with a sense of history. The fortress, dating back to Roman times, has witnessed the ebb and flow of centuries, from medieval rulers to the Ottoman and Austro-Hungarian empires.

Wander through the vibrant streets surrounding the fortress, where a mix of architectural styles reflects the city's diverse history. The Ferhadija Mosque, an Ottoman-era masterpiece with its graceful minaret, stands in juxtaposition to the austere beauty of the Orthodox Cathedral of Christ the Savior. This intersection of religious and cultural influences encapsulates the essence of Banja Luka – a city where diversity is celebrated.

Take a leisurely stroll along Gospodska Street, Banja Luka's main promenade, where charming cafes, boutiques, and historic buildings create a lively atmosphere. Imagine yourself seated at an outdoor cafe, sipping on locally brewed coffee, and watching the world go by. The laid-back vibe of Gospodska Street captures the essence of Banja Luka's spirit – a city that encourages you to savor the simple joys of life.

For a deeper dive into the city's history and culture, visit the Museum of Republika Srpska. Housed in a striking building with modern architecture, the museum offers exhibits that span the region's diverse heritage, from archaeological finds to contemporary art. As you explore, you'll gain insights into the complex history of Republika Srpska and the resilience of its people.

Banja Luka's iconic suspension bridge, the Vrbas Bridge, stretches across the river, connecting the two halves of the city. Picture yourself crossing this architectural marvel, where the gentle swaying of the bridge becomes a metaphor for the city's unhurried pace. The views of the Vrbas River and the surrounding greenery create a tranquil setting that invites contemplation.

As you explore the streets of Banja Luka, you'll encounter the Gospodarska Street Mosque, also known as the Ferhat Pasha Mosque. This Ottoman-era mosque, with its distinctive domes and minaret, is a place of serenity amidst the urban hustle. Step inside, where the coolness of the interior and the ornate decorations offer a respite from the outside world. The mosque, named after Ferhat Pasha, a prominent Ottoman statesman, is a testament to Banja Luka's multicultural history.

The Mladen Stojanović Park, nestled along the Vrbas River, provides a picturesque escape from the city's urban rhythm. Imagine yourself strolling along the tree-lined paths, where the scent of flowers mingles with the gentle murmur of the river. The park's green expanses and shaded areas invite you to relax, perhaps with a book or a leisurely picnic, as you soak in the natural beauty that defines Banja Luka.

For a taste of Banja Luka's culinary delights, explore the city's traditional eateries and cafes. Picture yourself in a rustic kafana, where the aroma of grilled meats and the sound of laughter create a convivial ambiance. Try local specialties such as Banjalučki ćevap, a variation of the minced meat kebab, or enjoy sogan-dolma, a dish featuring onions stuffed with a savory mixture of meat and rice. As you dine, you'll discover that Banja Luka's cuisine reflects the influences of Ottoman, Austro-Hungarian, and Balkan flavors.

Banja Luka's vibrant street art scene adds a contemporary touch to the city's cultural landscape. As you explore, you'll encounter colorful murals that depict scenes from local history, folklore, and modern life. Each mural becomes a piece of Banja Luka's evolving story, blending the old with the new in a visual celebration of creativity.

Venture to the Krajina Square, a bustling hub of activity where locals and visitors converge. The square, surrounded by cafes and shops, is a gathering point for events, festivals, and cultural performances. Picture yourself in the midst of a lively street festival, the air filled with music and the aroma of street food. The Krajina Square becomes a vibrant showcase of Banja Luka's dynamic spirit, where tradition and modernity coexist seamlessly.

A visit to the Banja Luka City Park reveals a tranquil oasis within the city. Imagine strolling along its paths, where sculptures, fountains, and floral displays create a serene ambiance. The park's centerpiece, the Petar Kočić Monument, pays homage to the renowned writer and political activist. As you sit on a bench, surrounded by greenery, you'll feel a sense of tranquility that contrasts with the lively energy of the city center.

For a cultural immersion, attend a performance at the Banski Dvor Cultural Center. This historic building, with its neoclassical architecture, hosts a variety of events, from concerts to theater productions. Picture yourself in the audience, surrounded by the elegance of the venue, as you enjoy a performance that showcases Banja Luka's vibrant artistic scene.

As the day transitions into evening, explore Banja Luka's nightlife along the Vrbas River. The riverside cafes and bars come alive, offering a relaxed setting to unwind and socialize. Picture yourself on a terrace overlooking the illuminated Vrbas Bridge, sipping on a local wine or cocktail. The rhythmic sounds of live music or the laughter of fellow patrons become the soundtrack to a laid-back evening in Banja Luka.

Consider staying in one of Banja Luka's boutique hotels or guesthouses, where the city's charm extends into your accommodation. Picture yourself in a room adorned with contemporary design, yet reflecting elements of Banja Luka's cultural heritage. As you retire for the night, the city's easygoing spirit lingers in the air, inviting you to embrace the unhurried rhythm of Banja Luka.

Banja Luka, the laid-back capital of Republika Srpska, becomes not just a destination but a sanctuary where time seems to slow down. As you bid farewell to this charming city, know that the memories of leisurely strolls, cultural discoveries, and moments of quiet reflection will stay with you. Banja Luka, with its warm hospitality and diverse heritage, invites you to experience life at its own pace – a pace that encourages you to savor each moment in a city where the past and present coalesce in a harmonious blend of relaxation and cultural richness.

Chapter 6
Tuzla – Salt of the Earth

Welcome to Tuzla, a city where the earth yields not only minerals but also a rich tapestry of history, culture, and warm hospitality. As you step into this Bosnian gem, nestled in the northeast of the country, you'll discover that Tuzla is more than a place – it's an invitation to explore the salt of the earth, both literally and metaphorically.

Begin your journey in the heart of Tuzla, where the Pannonian Plain meets the Dinaric Alps. The city unfolds along the banks of the Jala River, and the first glimpse of the Tuzla Salt Lake introduces you to one of the city's most iconic features. Picture yourself standing on the shores of this saline lake, where the reflections of the surrounding hills dance on the water's surface. The air is tinged with the faint scent of salt, a precursor to the unique experiences that Tuzla has in store.

The symbol of Tuzla, the Tuzla Salt Pans, takes you back to the city's ancient roots. Established during the Roman period, these salt pans are among the oldest in Europe, showcasing the city's legacy as a center for salt production. Imagine yourself walking along the wooden pathways that crisscross the pans, where the shimmering waters and the play of sunlight create a mesmerizing scene. The salt pans are not just a historical relic but a living testament to Tuzla's enduring connection with its natural resources.

A visit to the Salt Museum provides insights into the history of salt production in Tuzla. Picture yourself exploring the exhibits, where artifacts, tools, and multimedia presentations bring to life the centuries-old traditions of salt harvesting. The museum, housed in a historic building, allows you to trace the journey of salt from the pans to the tables, illustrating the significance of this mineral in shaping the city's identity.

Tuzla's Old Town, with its narrow streets and Ottoman-era architecture, offers a glimpse into the city's multicultural past. Wander through the cobbled alleys, where mosques, churches, and synagogues stand side by side, embodying the harmonious coexistence of different religious communities. As you explore, the call to prayer from the Aladža Mosque may harmonize with the bells from the Church of St. Nicholas, creating a symphony that resonates through the centuries.

One of the most captivating landmarks in Tuzla is the Wooden Footbridge, connecting the Old Town with the modern city center. Picture yourself crossing this historic bridge, where the Jala River flows beneath your feet. The bridge, dating back to the 18th century, exudes an understated charm, providing a picturesque vantage point to admire the fusion of old and new that defines Tuzla.

The Square of Freedom, a bustling hub in the city center, invites you to experience Tuzla's vibrant atmosphere. Imagine yourself surrounded by the lively energy of locals and visitors, exploring the shops, cafes, and cultural venues that line the square. The Freedom Fountain, with its playful water features, becomes a meeting point where people gather to chat, relax, and soak in the urban ambiance.

For a taste of Bosnian cuisine, explore the cafés and restaurants around the Square of Freedom. Picture yourself seated at an outdoor terrace, sampling local delicacies such as Tuzlanski ćevapi, a variation of minced meat kebabs, or burek, a savory pastry filled with meat or cheese. The flavors reflect the city's multicultural heritage, offering a culinary journey that mirrors Tuzla's diverse influences.

A leisurely stroll along the Korzo, the pedestrianized street in the city center, introduces you to Tuzla's modern side. Picture yourself window shopping, enjoying street performances, and stopping at trendy cafes for a cup of Bosnian coffee. The youthful energy of the Korzo blends seamlessly with the historical charm of the Old Town, creating a dynamic fusion that encapsulates Tuzla's evolving identity.

The Turalibeg's House, a well-preserved Ottoman-era residence, stands as a cultural gem in the heart of Tuzla. As you step inside, the aroma of aged wood and the intricate design of the interior transport you to a bygone era. Picture yourself exploring the rooms adorned with traditional Bosnian furnishings, imagining the lives of those who once inhabited this historic residence. The Turalibeg's House becomes a time capsule, preserving the elegance and simplicity of Tuzla's Ottoman past.

For a moment of reflection, visit the Meša Selimović Library, named after the renowned Bosnian writer. Picture yourself in the serene surroundings of the library, surrounded by books and the hushed whispers of knowledge seekers. The library, with its modern architecture, serves as a cultural oasis, inviting you to connect with literature, art, and the intellectual spirit that permeates Tuzla.

The Gradski Park, Tuzla's city park, unfolds as a green sanctuary within the urban landscape. Imagine yourself strolling along its shaded paths, where centuries-old trees provide a canopy of tranquility. The park's serene ambiance, complemented by fountains and sculptures, invites you to unwind and recharge amidst the natural beauty that graces Tuzla.

To delve into Tuzla's artistic scene, visit the Art Gallery of Bosnia and Herzegovina, Tuzla Branch. The gallery showcases contemporary art, providing a platform for local and international artists. Picture yourself exploring the exhibits, where paintings, sculptures, and multimedia installations offer a window into the diverse expressions of creativity. The gallery becomes a space where artistic dialogues intersect, mirroring Tuzla's openness to cultural exchange.

Tuzla's natural surroundings offer opportunities for outdoor enthusiasts to explore the beauty of the region. Imagine yourself hiking through the pristine landscapes of the Majevice Mountain, located just a short drive from the city. The mountain, with its lush forests and panoramic views, becomes a haven for those seeking a retreat into nature. Whether you embark on a challenging hike or simply savor the tranquility of the mountain air, Majevice provides a refreshing escape from the urban bustle.

As the sun sets over Tuzla, head to the Panonian Lakes, a series of artificial lakes created from former salt pans. Picture yourself by the water's edge, where the reflections of the sky and surrounding hills create a serene panorama. The lakes, now recreational areas, offer opportunities for boating, fishing, and simply enjoying the peaceful ambiance. The fading sunlight casts a warm glow on the lakes, inviting you to savor the beauty of Tuzla's landscapes.

Consider staying in one of Tuzla's boutique hotels or guesthouses, where the city's warmth extends into your accommodation. Picture yourself in a room adorned with contemporary design, offering comfort and style. As you retire for the night, the echoes of Tuzla's salt of the earth spirit linger, inviting you to reflect on the unique experiences and cultural richness of this Bosnian city.

Tuzla, with its salt pans, historical landmarks, and cultural vibrancy, becomes not just a destination but a journey into the heart of Bosnia and Herzegovina. As you bid farewell to this city, know that the memories of salt-laden air, historical discoveries, and the warmth of its people will accompany you. Tuzla, the salt of the earth, invites you to leave with a piece of its essence – a taste of the mineral that has shaped its identity and a connection to a city where the earth, the history, and the hospitality converge in a harmonious blend.

Chapter 7
Visegrad – A Town Steeped in History

Welcome to Višegrad, a town where history is etched into every stone, and the intertwining tales of empires and cultures unfold like the gentle flow of the Drina River. As you step into this Bosnian jewel, perched along the riverbanks, you'll find Višegrad to be a destination that transcends time, inviting you to wander through centuries of stories and immerse yourself in the cultural tapestry that defines this picturesque town.

The heart of Višegrad beats within the Mehmed Paša Sokolović Bridge, an architectural masterpiece that spans the Drina River. Picture yourself standing on this UNESCO World Heritage site, where the bridge's graceful arches reflect on the tranquil waters below. Built in the 16th century during the Ottoman era, the bridge is not merely a structure but a symbol of Višegrad's historical significance. As you gaze at the panoramic view, let the whispers of history transport you to an era when caravans crossed the river, and the bridge stood as a testament to engineering brilliance.

A visit to the Andrićgrad, a stone town named after the Nobel Prize-winning author Ivo Andrić, opens a portal to Višegrad's past. Picture yourself wandering through cobbled streets, where buildings adorned with Ottoman and Austro-Hungarian architectural elements create an ambiance reminiscent of the town's diverse heritage. The town, built as a tribute to Andrić and his literary legacy, becomes a living museum, where each corner reveals a story – a chapter from the rich history that has shaped Višegrad.

The Mehmed Paša Sokolović Bridge, often referred to simply as the Višegrad Bridge, is not just a crossing over the Drina but a meeting point of cultures and civilizations. Imagine yourself strolling across this iconic bridge, where the rhythmic sounds of your footsteps blend with the murmurs of the river below. As you reach the middle of the bridge, pause to take in the panoramic view of Višegrad, where the red-tiled roofs and minarets punctuate the landscape, echoing the town's Ottoman legacy.

The Višegrad Bridge is not only a witness to history but a key player in Ivo Andrić's masterpiece, "The Bridge on the Drina." As you traverse the stone path, let your imagination wander to the pages of this renowned novel, where the bridge serves as a silent observer of the triumphs and tribulations of Višegrad's residents. The bridge, both in literature and reality, becomes a symbol of endurance, connecting generations and preserving the essence of a town steeped in historical significance.

Wander through the cobbled streets of Višegrad's Old Town, where Ottoman-era structures such as the Mehmed Paša Sokolović Mosque and the Vilina Vlas Hotel stand as relics of the town's architectural legacy. Picture yourself exploring the mosque's courtyard, where the call to prayer once echoed through the air, creating a spiritual atmosphere that transcends time. The mosque, with its graceful minaret and adorned interiors, reflects the cultural richness of Višegrad during the Ottoman rule.

The Vilina Vlas Hotel, a building with a storied past, unveils another layer of Višegrad's history. Imagine standing before this grand structure, where the exterior exudes a sense of faded grandeur. The hotel, originally built as a residence for the Ottoman military governor, later became infamous as a site during the Bosnian War. Today, it serves as a reminder of the complexities that shape Višegrad's narrative, offering visitors a glimpse into the town's resilience and ability to heal.

Višegrad's vibrant marketplace, the Old Bazaar, invites you to experience the town's lively atmosphere. Picture yourself meandering through the stalls, where local artisans display handmade crafts, textiles, and traditional Bosnian products. Engage with the friendly vendors, perhaps purchasing a unique souvenir that reflects the authenticity of Višegrad's cultural heritage. The Old Bazaar becomes a melting pot of colors and sounds, embodying the town's centuries-old tradition of trade and commerce.

As you explore Višegrad, the memorial complex dedicated to Ivo Andrić becomes a pilgrimage for literature enthusiasts. Picture yourself amidst the serene surroundings, where a statue of Andrić stands as a tribute to the literary giant. The complex, encompassing the Andrićgrad and the Ivo Andrić Museum, offers a deeper understanding of the author's life and his profound connection to Višegrad. As you peruse the exhibits, you'll discover how the town and its people influenced Andrić's literary masterpieces.

The Višegrad Cemetery, a somber yet poignant site, unveils the layers of Višegrad's recent history. Imagine walking through rows of tombstones, each telling a story of lives lost and sacrifices made during times of conflict. The cemetery, with its peaceful ambiance, becomes a place for reflection and remembrance, inviting you to acknowledge the resilience of Višegrad's residents in the face of adversity.

The Andrićgrad, designed by filmmaker Emir Kusturica, stands as a cultural complex that celebrates Višegrad's historical and artistic heritage. Picture yourself in this stone town, where the architecture mirrors the styles of various epochs, from the Ottoman to the Austro-Hungarian. The streets, adorned with sculptures and artwork, become a visual feast, inviting you to explore the myriad influences that shape Višegrad's identity.

For a taste of traditional Bosnian cuisine, Višegrad's restaurants offer an array of dishes that reflect the town's multicultural heritage. Picture yourself in a cozy eatery, savoring local specialties such as ćevapi, japrak, and baklava. The flavors, influenced by Ottoman and Balkan culinary traditions, create a gastronomic experience that transports you to the heart of Višegrad's cultural fusion.

Višegrad's vibrant cultural scene often comes to life during festivals and events. Imagine yourself participating in the Andrićgrad Film and Theater Festival, where the town becomes a stage for artistic expressions from around the world. The lively atmosphere, filled with screenings, performances, and cultural exchanges, underscores Višegrad's commitment to fostering creativity and embracing diverse perspectives.

The Drina River, winding its way through Višegrad, becomes more than a geographical feature; it becomes a companion to your explorations. Picture yourself on a leisurely boat ride, where the gentle currents carry you along the scenic landscapes of Višegrad. The riverbanks, adorned with greenery and historic structures, offer a serene backdrop to your journey, allowing you to appreciate the town's beauty from a different perspective.

The House of Ivo Andrić, the Nobel laureate's childhood home, adds a personal touch to your exploration of Višegrad. Imagine standing in the rooms where Andrić spent his formative years, surrounded by the simplicity of 19th-century Bosnian life. The house, now a museum, preserves the atmosphere of a bygone era, allowing you to connect with the author's early influences and the cultural ambiance of Višegrad.

As the day turns to dusk, the Mehmed Paša Sokolović Bridge becomes a mesmerizing sight, illuminated by the warm glow of streetlights. Picture yourself on an evening stroll across the bridge, where the reflections on the river create a magical ambiance. The town, with its historic structures bathed in soft light, exudes a sense of tranquility that invites you to savor the timeless beauty of Višegrad.

Consider staying in one of Višegrad's charming guesthouses or boutique hotels, where the warmth of Bosnian hospitality becomes an integral part of your experience. Picture yourself in a room adorned with traditional décor, where the ambiance reflects the town's historical charm. As you retire for the night, the echoes of Višegrad's stories and the whispers of the Drina River accompany your dreams, creating a connection to a town that transcends time.

Višegrad, a town steeped in history, becomes not just a destination but a journey through the ages. As you bid farewell to this Bosnian gem, know that the echoes of the Višegrad Bridge, the cobbled streets, and the stories engraved in its stones will linger in your memories. Višegrad, with its cultural richness and timeless allure, invites you to become a part of its narrative – to walk its streets, traverse its bridge, and embrace the historical legacy that defines this enchanting town along the banks of the Drina River.

Chapter 8

Srebrenica – Remembering the Past

Welcome to Srebrenica, a place where the scars of history are etched into the landscape, and the weight of remembrance hangs in the air. As you enter this Bosnian town, nestled among the hills, you'll find Srebrenica to be a poignant destination that beckons travelers to bear witness to the tragic events of the past, to honor the lives lost, and to reflect on the enduring quest for justice and reconciliation.

Srebrenica's name resonates globally as a symbol of one of the darkest chapters in recent history – the Srebrenica genocide of 1995. The town, once a serene enclave surrounded by picturesque hills, became the epicenter of unimaginable atrocities during the Bosnian War. As you stand on the solemn grounds of the Memorial Center and Cemetery in Potočari, where thousands of victims are laid to rest, the weight of history becomes palpable.

The Srebrenica-Potočari Memorial Complex, established to commemorate the victims of the genocide, is a place of deep reflection and contemplation. Picture yourself walking through the cemetery, where rows of white tombstones stretch across the landscape. Each stone represents a life cut short, a story left untold. The enormity of the loss is profound, and the echoes of grief linger in the air, inviting visitors to pay their respects and acknowledge the human tragedy that unfolded here.

The haunting beauty of the landscape surrounding Srebrenica adds a layer of complexity to the town's narrative. Picture yourself surrounded by the lush greenery of the Drina Valley, where the hills bear witness to a history that cannot be erased. The natural serenity of the surroundings contrasts starkly with the weight of the past, creating an emotional dichotomy that defines Srebrenica's unique character.

The Dutchbat Memorial, situated within the Memorial Center, pays homage to the United Nations peacekeeping force that was stationed in

Srebrenica during the war. As you observe the memorial, adorned with plaques and inscriptions, you'll gain insight into the challenges faced by the Dutch soldiers who found themselves in an untenable position. The memorial becomes a testament to the complexities of international intervention and the sobering realization of the limitations faced by those who sought to prevent the unfolding tragedy.

The Gallery 11/07/95, located in the heart of Srebrenica, provides a comprehensive overview of the events leading up to the genocide. Imagine yourself in this gallery, surrounded by photographs, testimonials, and artifacts that chronicle the timeline of the war and its impact on the town and its people. The exhibits offer a deeply moving narrative, urging visitors to confront the harsh realities of the past and the collective responsibility to remember.

Srebrenica's Potocari War Memorial, adjacent to the cemetery, is a place of pilgrimage for those seeking to understand and commemorate the genocide. Picture yourself standing before the Wall of Names, where the identities of the victims are inscribed. As you run your fingers over the engraved names, the individuality of each person comes to the forefront – not just as a statistic, but as a human being with dreams, hopes, and a place within a community that was torn apart.

The Memorial Room within the gallery showcases personal items belonging to the victims, offering an intimate glimpse into their lives. Imagine yourself surrounded by the everyday objects – a pair of glasses, a toy, a piece of clothing – each telling a story of an individual who once inhabited the town. The Memorial Room becomes a sacred space, allowing visitors to connect with the humanity that transcends the overwhelming tragedy.

For a deeper understanding of the events leading up to the genocide, consider visiting the Srebrenica Genocide Memorial. Picture yourself in this solemn space, where photographs and narratives detail the systematic atrocities committed against the Bosniak population. The memorial becomes a stark reminder of the consequences of unchecked hatred and the urgent need for global solidarity to prevent such horrors from repeating.

Srebrenica's Old Town, with its Ottoman-era architecture and cobbled streets, offers a poignant contrast to the solemnity of the memorial sites. Picture yourself strolling through the narrow alleys, where the echoes of history blend with the vibrant life of the present. The Gazi Husrev-beg Mosque, dating back to the 16th century, stands as a testament to Srebrenica's multicultural heritage before the war, providing a glimpse into the town's diverse past.

To delve into the spiritual legacy of Srebrenica, visit the Gazi Mehmed Pasha Mosque, a structure that predates the war and continues to be a place of worship for the local community. Picture yourself within the mosque, where the tranquility of the interior contrasts with the tumultuous history that unfolded outside its walls. The mosque becomes a symbol of resilience, standing as a testament to the endurance of faith and community amidst the darkest of times.

Srebrenica's lively market, bustling with activity, invites you to engage with the local community and experience the town beyond its tragic history. Picture yourself exploring the stalls, where vendors offer fresh produce, handmade crafts, and traditional Bosnian goods. The market becomes a place of resilience, where the spirit of the community endures despite the weight of the past, demonstrating the human capacity for hope and renewal.

As you navigate through the streets of Srebrenica, the scent of traditional Bosnian cuisine wafts through the air. Picture yourself in a local restaurant, savoring dishes such as Bosanski lonac, japrak, or pita. The flavors, reminiscent of pre-war Bosnia, become a connection to the town's culinary heritage and a celebration of resilience through the continuity of cultural traditions.

Srebrenica's proximity to the Drina River invites you to explore the natural beauty that surrounds the town. Picture yourself on a tranquil boat ride along the river, where the gentle currents carry you through picturesque landscapes. The Drina, with its emerald green waters and verdant hills, provides a serene backdrop to your journey, offering a moment of solace amidst the challenging history of Srebrenica.

Consider staying in one of Srebrenica's guesthouses or accommodations, where the warmth of Bosnian hospitality becomes an integral part of your experience. Picture yourself in a room adorned with simple elegance, providing a respite from the emotional weight of the town's history. As you retire for the night, the quiet surroundings offer a space for contemplation, allowing you to process the profound impact of Srebrenica's past.

Srebrenica, a town forever marked by tragedy, becomes not just a destination but a sacred ground where remembrance and reflection intertwine. As you bid farewell to this solemn place, carry with you the stories of resilience, the faces engraved on the Wall of Names, and the collective responsibility to ensure that such atrocities never recur. Srebrenica, with its painful history and enduring spirit, invites you to honor the past, embrace the present, and contribute to a future built on the pillars of justice, remembrance, and hope.

Chapter 9
Bihac – Gateway to Una National Park

Welcome to Bihać, a charming town nestled on the banks of the Una River, where history, natural beauty, and vibrant culture converge to create a captivating destination. As you step into this Bosnian gem, you'll find Bihać to be not only a gateway to Una National Park but a destination in its own right, inviting travelers to explore its rich heritage, connect with the local community, and embark on adventures amid pristine landscapes.

Bihać's Old Town, with its cobbled streets and historic architecture, becomes a portal to the town's past. Picture yourself wandering through the narrow alleys, where Ottoman-era buildings coexist with Austro-Hungarian influences. The Fethija Mosque, a prominent landmark with its elegant minaret, stands as a testament to Bihać's multicultural history. As you explore the Old Town, the melodies of the adhan may intermingle with the lively chatter of locals, creating a harmonious ambiance that encapsulates Bihać's diverse heritage.

The Una River, flowing gracefully through the heart of Bihać, becomes a focal point for both locals and visitors. Picture yourself on the shores of the river, where the sound of cascading water and the lush greenery along the banks create a serene atmosphere. The Una, with its crystal-clear waters, invites you to partake in various water activities or simply unwind and enjoy the tranquility of the riverfront.

Bihać's captivating waterfront, known as the Šehitluci, offers a picturesque setting for a leisurely stroll or a riverside picnic. Imagine yourself seated at one of the cafes lining the riverbanks, sipping on Bosnian coffee, and watching the world go by. The Šehitluci becomes a gathering place where locals and travelers converge, creating a lively atmosphere that reflects the town's warmth and hospitality.

To delve into Bihać's historical tapestry, visit the Captain's Tower, a medieval fortress overlooking the Una River. Picture yourself ascending the stone steps of this iconic structure, where panoramic views of Bihać and the surrounding landscapes unfold. The Captain's Tower, with its medieval charm and strategic location, becomes a vantage point to contemplate the town's evolution through the centuries.

For a cultural immersion, explore Bihać's vibrant market, where the colors and aromas of fresh produce, local crafts, and traditional Bosnian goods create a lively tableau. Picture yourself navigating through the stalls, engaging with friendly vendors, and perhaps sampling regional delights like Bosanski lonac or ćevapi. The market becomes a microcosm of Bihać's community spirit, where the pulse of daily life is palpable.

Bihać's contemporary side comes to life along the pedestrianized King Tomislav Street, known locally as the Korzo. Picture yourself strolling along this bustling thoroughfare, where shops, cafes, and boutiques line the streets. The Korzo becomes a place to embrace the town's dynamic energy, with street performers, local artisans, and the aroma of freshly baked pastries contributing to its vibrant ambiance.

The Una National Park, a natural wonderland surrounding Bihać, beckons outdoor enthusiasts and nature lovers. Picture yourself embarking on a journey into the park, where dense forests, cascading waterfalls, and emerald-green rivers create a mesmerizing landscape. The Una River, with its series of waterfalls, including the iconic Štrbački Buk, becomes a focal point for exploration, offering opportunities for rafting, kayaking, or simply enjoying the beauty of untamed nature.

The Štrbački Buk waterfall, a stunning cascade within Una National Park, becomes a symbol of the park's raw beauty. Imagine standing on one of the viewpoints, where the thunderous sound of water echoes through the air. The waterfall, surrounded by pristine landscapes, invites you to marvel at the force of nature and immerse yourself in the serenity of the Una National Park.

For a scenic escape, visit the Martin Brod and Martin Brod II water-falls, where the Una River unfolds in a series of cascades. Picture your-self traversing the walking paths, with the sound of rushing water as your companion. The Martin Brod waterfalls offer a tranquil retreat, with shaded areas, picnic spots, and the opportunity to witness the diverse flo-ra and fauna that thrive in the park.

The Strbacki Buk and the nearby Štrbački Buk II waterfalls, accessi-ble by boat, become a part of your Una National Park exploration. Imag-ine yourself navigating the gentle currents, surrounded by lush greenery, as you approach these natural wonders. The boat ride becomes a sensory experience, allowing you to appreciate the untouched beauty of the Una River and its scenic surroundings.

The Una National Park is not only a haven for water-based activities but also a sanctuary for hikers and nature enthusiasts. Picture yourself on one of the park's hiking trails, where the dense forests, meadows, and di-verse wildlife create an immersive experience. The trails, varying in diffi-culty, offer opportunities to discover the park's hidden gems and witness the harmony between untouched nature and outdoor recreation.

The Una National Park's Una Kostela area, known for its tranquility and pristine landscapes, invites you to unwind and connect with nature. Imagine yourself at one of the scenic viewpoints, where the Una River meanders through the green expanse, reflecting the surrounding hills. The Una Kostela area becomes a retreat within the park, offering a peace-ful respite for those seeking solitude and contemplation.

To delve into the cultural heritage within Una National Park, visit the Rmanj Monastery, a historic site nestled in the park's enchanting landscapes. Picture yourself amidst the quietude of the monastery, sur-rounded by ancient stone walls and the fragrance of centuries-old trees. The Rmanj Monastery becomes a testament to the enduring connection between spirituality and nature, inviting you to explore the intertwining threads of culture and landscape.

Bihać's accommodation options, ranging from cozy guesthouses to comfortable hotels, provide a welcoming retreat after a day of exploration. Picture yourself in a room with views of the Una River or nestled within the town's historical quarter. As you retire for the night, the sounds of the river and the memories of Bihać's charm become an integral part of your Bosnian experience.

Bihać, as a gateway to Una National Park, transcends its role as a mere entry point; it becomes a destination of cultural richness, natural splendor, and warm hospitality. As you bid farewell to this Bosnian town, carry with you the echoes of the Una River, the charm of Bihać's Old Town, and the tranquility of the national park. Bihać, with its timeless allure and multifaceted experiences, invites you to not only discover its landscapes but to forge a connection with the heart of Bosnia and Herzegovina.

Chapter 10
Kravice Waterfalls – Nature's Spectacle

Welcome to Kravice Waterfalls, a breathtaking masterpiece crafted by nature itself, where cascading waters and lush greenery converge to create a symphony of sights and sounds. As you venture into this Bosnian natural wonder, you'll find Kravice to be more than just a series of waterfalls – it's a testament to the raw beauty that Bosnia and Herzegovina harbors within its landscapes.

Imagine approaching the waterfalls, the distant roar of water growing louder as you draw near. The anticipation builds, and suddenly, there it is – Kravice unfolds before you, a hidden gem nestled in the heart of the Neretva River basin. Picture yourself standing on the viewing platform, gazing at the spectacle that lies ahead. The Kravice Waterfalls, with their emerald-green pools and cascading curtains of water, become a mesmerizing sight that captivates the senses.

As you descend the path towards the waterfalls, the air becomes infused with the refreshing mist generated by the cascading water. Picture yourself feeling the cool droplets on your skin, a gentle reminder of the powerful natural forces at play. The ambiance is alive with the sounds of water crashing against rocks, creating a rhythm that resonates through the entire area.

The Kravice Waterfalls, often referred to as the "Niagara of Bosnia," become a haven for those seeking respite from the hustle of everyday life. Imagine finding a quiet spot along the riverbank, the soothing sounds of flowing water providing a backdrop to your moments of relaxation. The tranquility of Kravice invites you to unwind, to be present in the embrace of nature's beauty.

As you dip your toes into the cool waters of the river, the crystal-clear pools around the waterfalls beckon you to take a refreshing swim. Picture yourself immersing in the turquoise depths, surrounded by the verdant landscape. The experience is not just about the water; it's about connecting with the untamed beauty that defines Kravice and its natural allure.

To fully appreciate the grandeur of Kravice Waterfalls, consider taking a boat ride along the river. Picture yourself gently gliding through the emerald waters, the spray from the falls misting your face. The boat ride offers a unique perspective, allowing you to witness the waterfalls from different angles and marvel at the intricate rock formations carved by centuries of flowing water.

The lush green surroundings of Kravice contribute to its enchanting atmosphere. Picture yourself walking along the shaded pathways, where the vibrant colors of flora contrast against the limestone rocks. The flora in the area, including poplars, willows, and various shrubs, adds to the rich biodiversity that thrives in this haven of nature.

The biodiversity extends to the fauna as well, making Kravice a destination for birdwatchers and nature enthusiasts. Imagine spotting various bird species, from kingfishers to herons, as they gracefully navigate the skies above the waterfalls. The sounds of birdsong create a harmonious melody that complements the natural symphony of Kravice.

For a moment of solitude and reflection, find a quiet spot on one of the rocky outcrops surrounding the waterfalls. Picture yourself sitting there, the gentle hum of water creating a serene ambiance. The tranquility of Kravice becomes an invitation to connect with your surroundings, to appreciate the simplicity of nature's wonders.

The legends and folklore surrounding Kravice Waterfalls add a layer of mystique to this natural wonder. Imagine hearing local tales about mythical creatures inhabiting the hidden corners of the area or stories of ancient rituals that took place in the vicinity of the falls. The folklore becomes a part of Kravice's charm, weaving a narrative that resonates with the cultural fabric of Bosnia and Herzegovina.

The area around Kravice Waterfalls has also served as a backdrop for cultural and artistic events. Picture yourself attending a performance or a festival, where the cascading waters become a unique stage for artistic expressions. The blend of natural beauty and human creativity transforms Kravice into a dynamic venue that celebrates the convergence of art and nature.

A visit to the nearby village of Ljubuški offers insights into the local way of life. Picture yourself wandering through the charming streets, where traditional stone houses and welcoming locals create a warm and authentic atmosphere. The village becomes a gateway to the cultural richness of the region, providing a glimpse into the daily routines and customs that characterize life in this part of Bosnia and Herzegovina.

The accessibility of Kravice Waterfalls makes it an ideal day trip destination from cities like Mostar or Sarajevo. Imagine embarking on a scenic drive through the picturesque landscapes of Herzegovina, the anticipation building as you approach the waterfalls. The journey becomes a prelude to the natural spectacle that awaits, offering glimpses of the diverse beauty that defines the region.

Kravice Waterfalls, with their terraced limestone formations, offer a unique geological spectacle. Picture yourself exploring the intricate patterns and textures of the rocks, shaped over time by the relentless force of water. The geological wonders add an educational dimension to your visit, highlighting the dynamic processes that have sculpted the landscape of Kravice.

As you indulge in a picnic by the riverbanks, the panoramic views of Kravice become the backdrop to a leisurely meal. Picture yourself savoring local delicacies, perhaps brought from nearby villages, as you immerse yourself in the natural beauty that surrounds you. The experience of dining amidst such stunning scenery elevates the simple act of eating into a moment of pure bliss.

For those seeking a more adventurous experience, the cliffs around Kravice Waterfalls offer opportunities for rock climbing and exploration. Imagine navigating the rocky terrain, the adrenaline building as you ascend to higher vantage points. The panoramic views from the cliffs provide a different perspective of Kravice, showcasing its grandeur from a bird's-eye view.

Consider visiting Kravice Waterfalls during different seasons to witness the ever-changing face of this natural wonder. Picture yourself surrounded by the vibrant colors of autumn, with the foliage creating a tapestry of reds, yellows, and greens. Alternatively, envision the falls framed by the pristine white of winter, a tranquil and serene landscape that contrasts with the lively atmosphere of the warmer months.

As the day at Kravice comes to an end, imagine staying to witness the magical transformation of the waterfalls under the soft hues of the setting sun. The golden light bathes the landscape, casting a warm glow on the cascading waters. The transition from daylight to dusk adds a touch of enchantment to Kravice, turning it into a romantic and serene haven.

Kravice Waterfalls, with their timeless beauty and natural splendor, leave an indelible mark on all who are fortunate enough to experience them. As you bid farewell to this Bosnian jewel, carry with you the memories of the emerald-green pools, the soothing sounds of cascading water, and the sense of awe inspired by nature's grandeur. Kravice, with its simplicity and magnificence, invites you to appreciate the wonders that Bosnia and Herzegovina holds within its landscapes, reminding you of the enduring power and grace of the natural world.

Chapter 11
Blagaj – Where Rivers and Mysticism Converge

Welcome to Blagaj, a place where the beauty of nature harmonizes with centuries-old mysticism, creating a captivating tapestry that unfolds along the banks of the Buna River. As you step into this Bosnian town, you'll find Blagaj to be a destination that transcends the ordinary – a place where rivers, history, and spirituality converge, inviting travelers to immerse themselves in its unique blend of natural and cultural wonders.

Imagine approaching Blagaj, the scenic landscape slowly revealing itself as you meander along the road. The anticipation builds, and then, there it is – Blagaj comes into view, a picturesque town nestled at the foot of towering cliffs. The Buna River, with its crystal-clear waters, flows gracefully through the heart of Blagaj, setting the stage for a journey through history and mysticism.

As you walk along the riverbanks, the sight of the Buna Spring captivates your attention. Picture yourself standing before this natural wonder, where the Buna River emerges from a cavern at the base of a towering cliff. The spring, known as Vrelo Bune, is one of the largest and most powerful karst springs in Europe, creating a mesmerizing scene as it gushes forth with incredible force. The water, with its deep blue hue, becomes a symbol of purity and vitality, inviting you to contemplate the magic that lies within Blagaj's natural surroundings.

Perched above the Buna Spring, the Blagaj Tekija emerges as a testament to the spiritual legacy that permeates the town. Imagine yourself ascending the stone steps to this Dervish monastery, a structure that seamlessly blends with the natural contours of the cliff. The tekija, with its whitewashed walls and wooden accents, becomes a symbol of harmony between human architecture and the untamed beauty of the landscape.

The Blagaj Tekija, dating back to the 16th century, served as a place of spiritual retreat for Dervishes – Sufi Muslim mystics. Picture yourself entering the tekija, where the atmosphere exudes tranquility and contemplation. The simplicity of the interior, adorned with carpets and calligraphy, reflects the ascetic lifestyle embraced by the Dervishes, inviting you to experience the spiritual ambiance that lingers within these ancient walls.

The Dervishes, practitioners of Sufism, followed a path of spiritual enlightenment and self-discovery. As you stand within the Blagaj Tekija, imagine the echoes of prayers, music, and whirling dances that once reverberated through these halls. The tekija, with its centuries-old mysticism, becomes a portal to the spiritual dimensions of Blagaj, offering insight into the practices that have shaped the town's cultural identity.

For a moment of introspection, find a quiet spot within the tekija's courtyard, overlooking the Buna River. Picture yourself sitting there, the sound of flowing water providing a soothing backdrop to your reflections. The tekija's courtyard, shaded by ancient trees, becomes a sanctuary for contemplation, inviting you to connect with the spiritual essence that permeates Blagaj.

The Buna River, as it flows beneath the Blagaj Tekija, becomes a source of inspiration for both spiritual seekers and nature enthusiasts. Imagine taking a leisurely boat ride along the river, where the gentle currents carry you through the verdant landscapes of Blagaj. The boat ride offers a different perspective of the town, allowing you to appreciate the union of natural beauty and cultural heritage from the tranquility of the river.

The Old Bridge of Blagaj, an architectural gem that spans the Buna River, becomes a symbolic link between the town's historical and natural wonders. Picture yourself walking across this stone bridge, where the views of the tekija, cliffs, and river converge in a breathtaking panorama. The Old Bridge, with its arched design and rustic charm, becomes a testament to the enduring craftsmanship that defines Blagaj's architectural legacy.

As you explore the Old Town of Blagaj, the narrow streets and stone houses transport you to a bygone era. Picture yourself wandering through the alleys, where traditional Bosnian architecture meets the rustic charm of Ottoman influence. The Old Town becomes a living testament to Blagaj's rich history, inviting you to envision the lives of those who once inhabited these cobblestone streets.

The Clock Tower, standing tall in the heart of the Old Town, becomes a landmark that resonates with the passage of time. Imagine standing beneath this centuries-old structure, where the rhythmic ticking of the clock becomes a soundtrack to your exploration. The Clock Tower, with its ancient design, serves as a reminder that Blagaj's history is marked by the ebb and flow of time.

To delve into the local culture, visit the vibrant marketplace of Blagaj, where vendors showcase traditional crafts, fresh produce, and handmade goods. Picture yourself amidst the lively atmosphere, engaging with locals and perhaps sampling regional delicacies. The marketplace becomes a microcosm of Blagaj's community spirit, where the exchange of goods and camaraderie reflect the town's warm hospitality.

For a taste of Bosnian cuisine, Blagaj's local restaurants offer a delightful array of dishes influenced by the region's culinary traditions. Imagine yourself savoring specialties such as japrak, ćevapi, or burek, each bite a celebration of the rich flavors that define Bosnian gastronomy. The local eateries become a culinary journey, inviting you to indulge in the authentic tastes of Blagaj.

As the day transitions into evening, imagine dining at a riverside restaurant, the sun casting a warm glow over the Buna River. The soft murmur of flowing water and the distant call to prayer create a magical ambiance, turning your evening meal into a sensory experience. The riverside setting becomes a stage for moments of relaxation and connection with the rhythms of Blagaj.

Consider staying in one of Blagaj's guesthouses or boutique accommodations, where the charm of Bosnian hospitality becomes an integral part of your experience. Picture yourself in a room overlooking the Buna River or nestled within the Old Town, the echoes of the river and the tekija serving as a backdrop to your stay. As you retire for the night, the quiet surroundings offer a serene respite, allowing you to savor the timeless allure of Blagaj.

Blagaj, with its convergence of rivers and mysticism, becomes not just a destination but a journey through the essence of Bosnia and Herzegovina. As you bid farewell to this enchanting town, carry with you the memories of the Buna River, the spiritual ambiance of the tekija, and the echoes of history woven into the cobblestone streets. Blagaj, with its timeless allure and spiritual depth, invites you to embrace the interconnected threads of nature, history, and mysticism that define this Bosnian gem along the banks of the Buna.

Chapter 12
Pocitelj – A Step Back in Time

Welcome to Počitelj, a mesmerizing step back in time where the echoes of history resonate through cobbled streets, medieval structures, and the timeless beauty of the Neretva River. As you traverse the narrow alleys and ascend the stone steps of this Bosnian gem, you'll find Počitelj to be more than just a historic town – it's a living testament to the cultural richness and architectural legacy that defines Bosnia and Herzegovina.

Imagine approaching Počitelj, the town's silhouette emerging against the backdrop of the rugged Herzegovinian landscape. The imposing sight of the Počitelj Fortress, perched on a hilltop, captures your attention, hinting at the medieval splendor that awaits. Picture yourself crossing the Neretva River, the iconic silhouette of the Hajji Alija's Bridge welcoming you to a journey through the annals of time.

As you walk through Počitelj's Old Town, the allure of centuries past unfolds before you. Picture yourself navigating the labyrinthine alleys, where stone houses with terracotta roofs stand as silent witnesses to the town's enduring history. The Ottoman influence, evident in the architecture and design, transports you to an era when Počitelj was a flourishing center of culture and trade.

The Počitelj Fortress, a formidable structure overlooking the town, becomes your first destination. Imagine ascending the stone steps, the panoramic views of Počitelj and the Neretva Valley unfurling with each stride. The fortress, dating back to the medieval period, served as a strategic stronghold for various civilizations, from the Ottoman Turks to the Austro-Hungarian Empire. As you explore the fortress, envision the lives of those who once guarded this elevated vantage point and the pivotal role it played in the region's history.

The Sahat-kula, or clock tower, within the fortress complex becomes a focal point of your exploration. Picture yourself standing before this centuries-old timepiece, its weathered facade telling tales of bygone eras. The Sahat-kula, with its Ottoman architectural elements, serves as a visual reminder of Počitelj's cultural amalgamation and the passage of time etched into the town's skyline.

As you descend from the fortress, the sound of the Neretva River draws you towards the heart of Počitelj. The Hajji Alija's Bridge, a symbol of the town's connection to trade routes, becomes a picturesque crossing over the serene waters. Picture yourself standing on the bridge, contemplating the reflections of Počitelj's ancient stone structures mirrored in the river below. The bridge becomes a bridge not only over water but over the centuries, linking the past with the present.

To delve into the artistic legacy of Počitelj, visit the Hadži-Alija Mosque and its accompanying madrasa. Imagine entering the mosque courtyard, where the soft sunlight filters through ancient trees, creating a tranquil atmosphere. The mosque, with its elegant minaret and ornate details, becomes a testament to the town's cultural and religious heritage. The adjacent madrasa, once a center of learning, invites you to imagine the echoes of scholarly discussions that once resonated within its walls.

Počitelj's Clock Tower, located near the mosque, adds to the town's architectural charm. Picture yourself standing in the shadow of this slender tower, its intricate design and functioning clock serving as a visual marker of Počitelj's meticulous craftsmanship. The Clock Tower, with its timeless elegance, stands as a testament to the town's commitment to preserving its heritage.

As you explore the Hadži-Alija Mosque and its surroundings, imagine engaging with local artisans who continue to practice traditional crafts. The workshops, tucked away in corners of the Old Town, become windows into the artistry that has been passed down through generations. Picture yourself observing skilled hands shaping clay, carving wood, or weaving intricate patterns, each creation reflecting the town's dedication to preserving its cultural identity.

The Počitelj hamam, an Ottoman-era bathhouse, becomes another stop on your journey through the town's historical tapestry. Picture yourself entering the hamam, where the architectural remnants and arched windows evoke images of a bygone era. The hamam, once a place of ritual cleansing and socialization, offers a glimpse into the daily lives of those who inhabited Počitelj during the Ottoman period.

As you stroll through Počitelj's Old Town, the aroma of Bosnian coffee wafts through the air, drawing you into local cafes and teahouses. Picture yourself seated in a courtyard, sipping on coffee, and absorbing the ambiance of centuries-old stones beneath your feet. The cafes become gathering spaces where locals and visitors alike come together, fostering a sense of community that transcends time.

For a panoramic perspective of Počitelj, imagine climbing the minaret of the Hadži-Alija Mosque. As you ascend, the town unfolds beneath you, revealing the intricate network of roofs, alleys, and courtyards. From this vantage point, Počitelj becomes a living canvas, each structure telling a story that contributes to the overall masterpiece of the town.

Počitelj's artistic spirit extends to the galleries and ateliers scattered throughout the Old Town. Picture yourself entering these spaces, where contemporary artists showcase their work inspired by the town's history and natural surroundings. The galleries become a testament to Počitelj's enduring appeal, capturing the imaginations of artists who find inspiration in its timeless charm.

As you continue your exploration, envision participating in one of Počitelj's cultural events or festivals. Picture yourself amidst lively celebrations, where traditional music, dance, and crafts bring the town to life. The events become a bridge between past and present, allowing you to experience Počitelj not only as a historical destination but as a vibrant community that continues to celebrate its cultural heritage.

To savor the flavors of Počitelj, indulge in local delicacies at one of the town's restaurants or taverns. Picture yourself seated at a table, the aroma of freshly prepared dishes filling the air. Bosnian specialties, such as japrak, ćevapi, and pita, become a culinary journey through the region's rich gastronomic traditions. The meals become moments of indulgence, inviting you to savor the tastes that define Počitelj's culinary identity.

Consider staying in one of Počitelj's charming guesthouses, where the authentic ambiance of the Old Town becomes an integral part of your experience. Picture yourself in a room with traditional decor, the sounds of the Neretva River serving as a soothing soundtrack to your stay. As you retire for the night, the quiet surroundings offer a sense of serenity, allowing you to fully immerse yourself in the timelessness of Počitelj.

Počitelj, with its cobbled streets, medieval architecture, and cultural depth, becomes a sanctuary for those seeking a step back in time. As you bid farewell to this Bosnian gem, carry with you the images of the Neretva River, the echoes of centuries past within the fortress walls, and the artistic spirit that animates the town. Počitelj, with its timeless allure, invites you to traverse the bridge between history and contemporary life, urging you to appreciate the beauty that emerges when past and present coexist in harmony.

Chapter 13

National Museum of Bosnia and Herzegovina – Unveiling the Past

Welcome to the National Museum of Bosnia and Herzegovina, an institution that stands as a guardian of the nation's rich cultural heritage and a storyteller of the past. As you step into this cultural haven, you'll find more than just artifacts and exhibits – the museum becomes a portal through time, inviting you to unravel the layers of Bosnia and Herzegovina's history, art, and identity.

Imagine approaching the National Museum, an architectural gem nestled in the heart of Sarajevo. The building itself, with its Austro-Hungarian influences, becomes a testament to the diverse cultural threads that weave through the country's history. Picture yourself ascending the grand staircase, the museum's facade a visual prelude to the treasures that lie within.

The National Museum, founded in 1888, stands as one of the oldest and most significant cultural institutions in Bosnia and Herzegovina. As you enter, the scent of aged wood and historical resonance greets you, setting the stage for a journey through time. The museum, with its vast collection spanning archaeology, ethnology, art, and natural history, becomes a comprehensive exploration of the nation's multifaceted identity.

Begin your journey in the Archaeology section, where artifacts from prehistoric to medieval times unveil the ancient civilizations that once thrived in the region. Picture yourself standing before Neolithic pottery, Roman sculptures, and medieval manuscripts, each item a silent witness to the ebb and flow of history. The Archaeology section becomes a walk through the epochs, connecting you to the roots of Bosnia and Herzegovina's cultural tapestry.

The Ethnology section of the museum offers a glimpse into the traditions, lifestyles, and crafts that have shaped the diverse communities within Bosnia and Herzegovina. Imagine immersing yourself in exhibits that showcase regional attire, traditional music instruments, and everyday objects infused with cultural significance. The Ethnology section becomes a living narrative of the nation's customs, illustrating the resilience and richness of Bosnia and Herzegovina's cultural mosaic.

The Art collection within the National Museum transports you through the centuries, presenting masterpieces that reflect the evolution of Bosnian and Herzegovinian artistic expression. Picture yourself standing before works of renowned painters, sculptors, and craftsmen whose creations have left an indelible mark on the country's artistic landscape. The Art section becomes a visual journey, where brushstrokes and forms convey the emotions, stories, and aspirations of generations past.

One of the highlights of the National Museum is the Sarajevo Haggadah, a medieval Jewish manuscript of illuminated Hebrew text. Imagine standing before this cultural treasure, carefully turning the pages to reveal intricate illustrations and calligraphy. The Sarajevo Haggadah, a symbol of religious tolerance and shared heritage, becomes a testament to the coexistence of diverse communities within Bosnia and Herzegovina.

The Natural History section of the museum invites you to explore the country's diverse ecosystems, from the lush landscapes of the Dinaric Alps to the pristine waters of the Neretva River. Picture yourself marveling at taxidermy specimens of native wildlife and examining geological formations that tell the story of Bosnia and Herzegovina's natural wonders. The Natural History section becomes a journey into the country's ecological wealth, fostering an appreciation for the delicate balance between nature and civilization.

As you navigate the museum's halls, imagine encountering interactive displays, multimedia presentations, and immersive exhibits that bring history to life. The National Museum of Bosnia and Herzegovina goes beyond static artifacts; it employs innovative storytelling methods to engage visitors and provide a dynamic, participatory experience. The museum becomes a space where history is not confined to the past but resonates in the present, inviting you to actively connect with the narratives it unfolds.

Consider attending one of the museum's events, lectures, or workshops that delve into various aspects of Bosnia and Herzegovina's cultural heritage. Picture yourself in a gathering of fellow enthusiasts, engaging in discussions with experts, and perhaps participating in hands-on activities that deepen your understanding of the nation's rich legacy. The National Museum becomes a hub of intellectual and cultural exchange, fostering connections between visitors and the wealth of knowledge it holds.

The National Museum of Bosnia and Herzegovina also plays a pivotal role in preserving and restoring cultural artifacts that have faced the challenges of time and conflict. Picture yourself witnessing the meticulous work of conservationists and restorers, breathing new life into ancient manuscripts, delicate textiles, and weathered sculptures. The museum becomes a guardian not only of Bosnia and Herzegovina's past but of the ongoing efforts to safeguard its cultural treasures for future generations.

To fully appreciate the significance of the National Museum, consider exploring its surroundings in Sarajevo. Picture yourself strolling through the city's historic neighborhoods, where Austro-Hungarian architecture and Ottoman influences coalesce. Sarajevo, with its vibrant atmosphere and diverse cultural influences, becomes the backdrop against which the narratives within the National Museum come to life.

The National Museum of Bosnia and Herzegovina is more than a repository of artifacts; it serves as a cultural bridge that connects the diverse communities within the country. Imagine engaging with locals who share their perspectives on the exhibits, adding personal stories and insights that enrich your understanding of Bosnia and Herzegovina's history. The museum becomes a space for cultural exchange, fostering connections that transcend boundaries and promote a deeper appreciation for the nation's heritage.

For those seeking a contemplative moment, consider finding a quiet corner within the museum's courtyard or gardens. Picture yourself surrounded by the greenery, the sounds of birdsong creating a serene ambiance. The outdoor spaces become an extension of the museum's allure, inviting you to reflect on the stories, art, and history that have unfolded within its walls.

As you bid farewell to the National Museum of Bosnia and Herzegovina, carry with you the images of ancient artifacts, the echoes of diverse cultures, and the sense of connection to the nation's past. The museum becomes a vessel through which you've navigated the intricate narratives that define Bosnia and Herzegovina's identity. The National Museum, with its dedication to preserving and sharing the nation's cultural wealth, leaves an indelible mark on your journey, inspiring a deeper appreciation for the threads that weave the fabric of this captivating country.

Chapter 14
Bosnian Cuisine – A Culinary Odyssey

Welcome to the culinary heart of Bosnia and Herzegovina, where each dish tells a story, and every bite is a journey through centuries of tradition, culture, and flavors. Bosnian cuisine, a fusion of Ottoman, Austro-Hungarian, and Balkan influences, is a culinary odyssey that beckons you to explore the diverse and delicious tapestry of this enchanting country.

Imagine strolling through the bustling markets of Sarajevo, where the aroma of grilled meats, freshly baked bread, and aromatic spices fills the air. The rich tapestry of Bosnian cuisine begins here, in the lively bazaars and local eateries that line the streets. As you navigate the bustling marketplaces, envision the vibrant displays of colorful produce, the sizzle of grills, and the inviting aromas that draw you closer to the culinary wonders of Bosnia and Herzegovina.

To embark on your culinary odyssey, start with Ćevapi, Bosnia's iconic dish and a staple of Balkan cuisine. Picture yourself in a local kafana, savoring these grilled minced meat sausages, usually made from a blend of beef and lamb. The dish is often served with somun, a traditional Bosnian flatbread, and accompanied by finely chopped onions and a dollop of kajmak, a creamy dairy spread. The marriage of smoky, succulent meat with the pillowy bread and creamy kajmak creates a symphony of flavors that is quintessentially Bosnian.

Japrak, grape leaves stuffed with a savory mixture of minced meat and rice, is another culinary gem that invites you to savor the essence of Bosnian cuisine. Picture yourself at a family table, where these rolled parcels are lovingly prepared and served alongside a generous dollop of yogurt. The grape leaves, infused with the flavors of the filling and a hint of tanginess from the yogurt, offer a delightful balance that reflects the intricate culinary heritage of Bosnia and Herzegovina.

As you journey deeper into the culinary landscape, imagine the comforting aroma of Bosanski Lonac wafting through the air. This traditional Bosnian pot stew is a hearty blend of meats, vegetables, and spices, slow-cooked to perfection. Picture yourself in a rustic setting, surrounded by the warmth of family and friends, as you indulge in the rich flavors and tender textures of this beloved dish. Bosanski Lonac embodies the essence of Bosnian hospitality, inviting you to partake in a communal experience that transcends the act of eating.

Burek, a flaky pastry filled with minced meat, cheese, or potatoes, is a savory delight that reflects the Ottoman influence on Bosnian cuisine. Imagine yourself in a local bakery, watching as skilled hands meticulously layer thin sheets of dough and generously fill them with savory goodness. Burek, often enjoyed with yogurt, becomes a culinary treasure that showcases the artistry of Bosnian bakers and the delectable fusion of flavors that defines this beloved dish.

For a taste of Bosnia's freshwater bounty, imagine indulging in a plate of Pastrmka, grilled trout sourced from the pristine rivers that meander through the country. Picture yourself at a riverside restaurant, the serene waters providing a backdrop as you savor the delicate flavors of the freshly caught trout. Pastrmka, often seasoned with local herbs and lemon, offers a culinary connection to Bosnia's natural abundance and the purity of its waterways.

Pita, a type of Bosnian pie, is a savory delicacy that varies in fillings and preparations across the country. Envision yourself in a village kitchen, where layers of thin dough are skillfully assembled with fillings such as cheese, potatoes, or pumpkin. The aroma of baking pita fills the air, and as you take your first bite, the layers of flaky pastry reveal a symphony of flavors that encapsulate the essence of Bosnian home cooking.

To satisfy your sweet tooth, Bosnian desserts offer a delectable array of options. Baklava, a rich and sweet pastry made of layers of filo dough, nuts, and honey, is a timeless treat that embodies the sweet side of Bosnian culinary craftsmanship. Imagine yourself in a traditional Bosnian café, where the golden layers of baklava are served alongside a cup of strong Bosnian coffee. The combination of sweet and bitter creates a sensory experience that encapsulates the complexity of Bosnian flavors.

Tufahija, a traditional Bosnian dessert, offers a sweet celebration of local ingredients. Picture yourself indulging in this delightful treat made of poached quinces, walnuts, and sugar, all topped with a dollop of whipped cream. Tufahija, with its harmonious blend of textures and flavors, is a testament to Bosnia's bounty of seasonal fruits and the artistry of its dessert makers.

Coffee, an integral part of Bosnian social life, is an experience in itself. Envision yourself at a traditional Bosnian kafana, sipping on a cup of strong, aromatic Bosnian coffee served in a džezva, a traditional coffee pot. The ritual of Bosnian coffee, often accompanied by rahat lokum (Turkish delight), becomes a cultural experience that invites you to linger, converse, and savor the rich depths of Bosnian hospitality.

Rakija, a fruit brandy that holds a special place in Bosnian tradition, is a beverage that invites you to partake in the country's convivial spirit. Picture yourself in a rural setting, where a local distiller crafts this strong spirit from fruits such as plums or grapes. As you raise your glass for a toast, the robust flavors of rakija become a celebration of Bosnia's distilling heritage and a warm invitation to join in the camaraderie of its people.

To fully immerse yourself in the culinary odyssey of Bosnia and Herzegovina, consider participating in a cooking class or food tour. Picture yourself in a kitchen, learning the intricacies of crafting Bosnian delicacies from passionate local chefs. The hands-on experience becomes a culinary adventure that not only tantalizes your taste buds but also provides insight into the cultural nuances of Bosnian gastronomy.

As you explore the diverse flavors of Bosnian cuisine, envision the culinary traditions that have been passed down through generations. The meals become more than just sustenance; they are a living expression of Bosnia and Herzegovina's history, culture, and the enduring spirit of its people. Whether you find yourself in a rustic village or a vibrant city, Bosnian cuisine becomes a journey that transcends time and invites you to savor the essence of this captivating country, one delicious bite at a time.

Chapter 15
Outdoor Adventures – Hiking

Welcome to the wild and untamed beauty of Bosnia and Herzegovina, where outdoor adventures beckon the intrepid traveler to explore lush landsteps, meandering rivers, and rugged mountain terrains. This chapter invites you to embrace the thrill of outdoor escapades, from exhilarating hikes to heart-pounding rafting experiences, as you discover the natural wonders that define this captivating country.

Picture yourself standing at the trailhead of the Via Dinarica, a long-distance hiking route that traverses the Dinaric Alps and showcases the diverse landscapes of Bosnia and Herzegovina. As you lace up your hiking boots, imagine embarking on a journey that unfolds through dense forests, alpine meadows, and rocky peaks. The Via Dinarica, a trail connecting local villages and offering breathtaking vistas, becomes a path of discovery that invites you to immerse yourself in the raw beauty of Bosnia's untamed wilderness.

The hiking trails in Bosnia and Herzegovina cater to various skill levels, ensuring that both seasoned trekkers and casual enthusiasts can find a route that suits their preferences. Picture yourself meandering through the pristine Una National Park, where hiking trails reveal cascading waterfalls, crystal-clear rivers, and vibrant flora. The rhythmic sound of your footsteps becomes a harmonious symphony with nature, allowing you to connect with the tranquility that pervades Bosnia's untouched landscapes.

For those seeking an immersive mountain experience, envision yourself exploring the Sutjeska National Park, home to the imposing peaks of Maglić and Volujak. As you ascend through ancient forests and alpine meadows, the panoramic views from the summits become a reward for your trekking efforts. The Sutjeska National Park, with its diverse ecosystems and rich biodiversity, becomes a haven for outdoor enthusiasts who yearn to lose themselves in the grandeur of Bosnia's natural wonders.

As the day unfolds, consider resting in a mountain hut or a cozy guesthouse, where the warmth of Bosnian hospitality awaits. Picture yourself sharing stories with fellow hikers, savoring local cuisine, and basking in the camaraderie of like-minded adventurers. The mountain refuges become not just shelters but hubs of community, where the shared love for outdoor exploration creates bonds that transcend language and cultural barriers.

For those who crave the thrill of whitewater adventures, imagine yourself on the foaming rapids of the Neretva River. Rafting in Bosnia and Herzegovina is an exhilarating experience that combines the rush of adrenaline with the stunning beauty of the river canyons. Picture yourself navigating through the twists and turns of the Neretva, the cool spray of water invigorating your senses as you conquer the river's challenges. Rafting becomes a dynamic exploration of Bosnia's untamed waterways, offering a unique perspective of the country's diverse landscapes.

The Tara River, with its emerald waters and deep canyons, presents another rafting paradise in Bosnia and Herzegovina. Envision yourself rafting through the Tara River Canyon, the second deepest canyon in the world, surrounded by sheer cliffs and pristine wilderness. The thrill of conquering the rapids is complemented by moments of tranquility as you float through the calmer stretches, providing a balanced and immersive rafting experience.

Beyond hiking and rafting, Bosnia and Herzegovina offers a spectrum of outdoor activities that cater to every adventurer's taste. Imagine exploring the scenic countryside on a mountain bike, the winding trails guiding you through charming villages and panoramic vistas. Cycling becomes a leisurely yet invigorating way to connect with the landscapes, allowing you to discover hidden gems and experience the rhythmic pulse of rural life.

For those who seek a more serene outdoor experience, envision a leisurely kayak journey on the Vrbas River. As you paddle through the calm waters, the surrounding hills and lush greenery create a tranquil ambiance. Kayaking becomes a gentle exploration, offering a different perspective of Bosnia's natural beauty while allowing you to enjoy moments of reflection and connection with the serene river environment.

The mystical allure of Bosnia and Herzegovina extends to its cave systems, where spelunking enthusiasts can uncover subterranean wonders. Picture yourself descending into the depths of the Vjetrenica Cave, one of the largest caves in the Dinaric Alps. As you explore the intricate formations and underground chambers, the cave becomes a realm of mystery and discovery, inviting you to unravel the secrets hidden beneath Bosnia's surface.

Imagine embarking on a paragliding adventure, soaring high above the landscapes of Bjelašnica or Jahorina. The feeling of weightlessness, the wind in your hair, and the panoramic views unfolding beneath you create a sense of freedom and exhilaration. Paragliding becomes a thrilling way to witness the vast expanses of Bosnia and Herzegovina from a bird's-eye perspective, adding a touch of adrenaline to your outdoor escapades.

For those seeking a more contemplative outdoor experience, envision yourself at one of Bosnia's tranquil lakes, surrounded by serene landscapes. Jablanica Lake, nestled between mountains and forests, becomes a haven for relaxation and reflection. Picture yourself on the shores of the lake, the calm waters reflecting the surrounding peaks, as you unwind and soak in the peaceful ambiance that defines Bosnia's idyllic natural settings.

As your outdoor adventures in Bosnia and Herzegovina unfold, consider engaging with local guides and communities. Imagine learning about the region's flora, fauna, and cultural heritage from those who call these landscapes home. Local guides become storytellers, sharing their knowledge and passion for the outdoors, adding depth and authenticity to your exploration of Bosnia's natural wonders.

In the evenings, after a day of outdoor exploration, envision yourself indulging in the warmth of a traditional Bosnian meal. Picture a table laden with grilled meats, fresh vegetables, and aromatic herbs, a feast that replenishes your energy and satisfies your appetite. The shared tales of the day's adventures become an integral part of the dining experience, creating a sense of camaraderie that transcends the physical exertion of outdoor pursuits.

As you conclude your outdoor odyssey in Bosnia and Herzegovina, carry with you the images of towering peaks, rushing rivers, and untouched wilderness. The memories of hiking through ancient forests, rafting down exhilarating rapids, and connecting with the landscapes on two wheels become souvenirs of a journey that celebrates the untamed beauty of this captivating country. Bosnia and Herzegovina, with its diverse outdoor offerings, becomes an adventurer's paradise, inviting you to explore, discover, and be inspired by the breathtaking landscapes that define its soul.

Appendix
Resources and Useful Information

As your journey through Bosnia and Herzegovina unfolds, it's essential to have access to helpful resources and information that enhance your travel experience. Here, we provide a comprehensive guide to resources that will assist you in navigating the diverse landscapes, rich cultural heritage, and unique experiences that this captivating country has to offer.

1. Travel Essentials:

- **Visa Information:** Check the official website of the Bosnia and Herzegovina Embassy or Consulate in your country for visa requirements and application procedures.
- **Currency:** The official currency is the Convertible Mark (BAM). Familiarize yourself with the current exchange rates and consider withdrawing local currency upon arrival.
- **Language:** The official languages are Bosnian, Croatian, and Serbian. English is widely spoken in tourist areas, but it's helpful to learn a few basic phrases in the local language.
- **Weather:** Bosnia and Herzegovina experiences a continental climate. Check the weather forecast for the specific regions you plan to visit, as temperatures can vary.

2. Transportation:

- **Public Transportation:** Utilize the country's well-connected bus and train network for cost-effective and efficient travel between cities.
- **Car Rentals:** Consider renting a car for more flexibility, especially if you plan to explore remote areas or the countryside.

- **Taxis:** Use reputable taxi services and agree on the fare before starting your journey.
- **Local Apps:** Download local transportation apps for real-time information and navigation assistance.

3. Accommodation:

- **Booking Platforms:** Use reliable online platforms such as Booking.com, Airbnb, or local hotel websites to secure accommodations.
- **Hostels:** Explore budget-friendly hostels for a sociable and affordable stay.
- **Guesthouses:** Experience Bosnian hospitality by staying in charming guesthouses, particularly in smaller towns.

4. Safety and Health:

- **Emergency Numbers:** Save the local emergency numbers for quick assistance.
- **Health Insurance:** Ensure you have comprehensive travel insurance that covers medical emergencies.
- **Vaccinations:** Check with your healthcare provider for recommended vaccinations before traveling.

5. Cultural Etiquette:

- **Respect Local Customs:** Familiarize yourself with Bosnian customs and show respect for local traditions.
- **Dress Modestly:** When visiting religious sites, dress modestly out of respect for the local culture.
- **Tipping:** Tipping is appreciated but not mandatory. Round up the bill or leave a small tip for good service.

6. Tourist Information Centers:

- **Locations:** Identify tourist information centers in major cities and tourist hotspots for maps, brochures, and local insights.
- **Guided Tours:** Inquire about guided tours and excursions for a deeper understanding of specific destinations.

7. Internet and Communication:

- **SIM Cards:** Purchase a local SIM card for affordable data and communication.
- **Free Wi-Fi:** Many cafes, restaurants, and accommodations offer free Wi-Fi.
- **Translation Apps:** Download translation apps for assistance with the local language.

8. Photography and Filming:

- **Respect Privacy:** Ask for permission before photographing individuals, especially in rural areas.
- **Scenic Spots:** Capture the stunning landscapes but be mindful of local regulations regarding photography.

9. Environmental Responsibility:

- **Waste Disposal:** Dispose of waste responsibly and support eco-friendly initiatives.
- **Wildlife Interaction:** Avoid disturbing wildlife and adhere to conservation guidelines.
- **Cultural Sites:** Respect historical and cultural sites by following designated paths and rules.

10. Local Events and Festivals:

- **Event Calendars:** Check local event calendars for festivals, concerts, and cultural events during your visit.
- **Participation:** Engage with local celebrations to immerse yourself in Bosnian culture.

11. Language and Travel Apps:

- **Translation Apps:** Utilize language translation apps for seamless communication.
- **Maps and Navigation:** Download offline maps or use navigation apps to navigate cities and remote areas.

12. Further Reading:

- **Books and Guides:** Explore literature about Bosnia and Herzegovina's history, culture, and travel experiences.
- **Blogs and Travel Journals:** Gain insights from fellow travelers who have shared their experiences online.

13. Contacts:

- **Embassies and Consulates:** Keep contact information for your country's embassy or consulate in Bosnia and Herzegovina.
- **Emergency Contacts:** Save local emergency contacts, including police, medical, and embassy numbers.

14. Feedback and Suggestions:

- **Tourist Feedback:** Share your experiences with local businesses, accommodations, and attractions.
- **Suggestions:** Provide constructive feedback to contribute to the improvement of the local tourism industry.

15. Social Media and Online Communities:

- **Online Forums:** Join travel forums and social media groups to connect with fellow travelers and gain valuable insights.
- **Local Influencers:** Follow local influencers and travel bloggers for real-time updates and recommendations.

Armed with this comprehensive guide, you are well-equipped to embark on a memorable journey through Bosnia and Herzegovina. May your travels be filled with discovery, cultural enrichment, and the joy of exploring the diverse landscapes that make this country a truly unique destination. Safe travels!

Printed in Great Britain
by Amazon